Home Bible Study

By

Johnie Edwards

© **Truth Publications, Inc. 2018. Second Printing.** All rights reserved. No part of this book may be reproduced in any form without written permission from the publisher. Printed in the United States of America.

ISBN 10: 1-58427-309-7

ISBN 13: 978-1-58427-309-7

First Printing: 2010

Truth Publications, Inc.
CEI Bookstore
220 S. Marion St., Athens, AL 35611
855-492-6657
sales@truthpublications.com
www.truthbooks.com

Table of Contents

		Page
Lesson 1:	Authority in Religion	7
Lesson 2:	God's Plan for Saving Man	11
Lesson 3:	The Church	15
Lesson 4:	The Worship of the Church	19

Home Bible Study

We are happy to have you study with us for the next few weeks. These *Home Bible Study* lessons are simple and scriptural. They do not contain the wisdom of men, but the wisdom of God. They have been prepared, with great care and concern, for the salvation of the souls of men.

Please take your Bible, look up the Scriptures listed, fill in the blanks, and answer any questions. These lessons are based on the New King James Version of the Bible. Remember that the Bible is the word of God and that we can be saved only by studying it, believing it, and doing what it teaches us to do.

All Scripture is given by inspiration of God, and is profitable for doctrine, for reproof, for correction, for instruction in righteousness, that the man of God may be complete, thoroughly equipped for every good work (2 Tim. 3:16-17).

Be diligent to present yourself approved to God, a worker who does not need to be ashamed, rightly dividing the word of truth (2 Tim. 2:15).

If you have any questions or comments to make, write them in the appropriate place so you can remember to mention them at the right time. Write your name on your material as you will want to keep it to use for further study later.

Name: _____

Date: _____

Place of Study: _____

A Suggestion Regarding the Use of This Material

1. It is recommended that a time be set for teaching the Home Bible Study either in your home or the home of your student(s).

2. It is good to cover only one lesson per week and that you stay with the material.

3. The study is designed for class participation.

4. Suggest an area like the dining room table for this study.

5. A novice in the word may have difficulty locating Bible passages. We suggest that you provide each student with a Bible (perhaps a pew Bible) and give them the page numbers as you call out the Bible verses.

6. Seasoned Christians would do well to study this material, in preparing to teach others (2 Tim. 2:2).

Lesson 1
Authority in Religion

Introduction
1. Most of the religious division is caused by a lack of respect for the word of God and the authority of Christ.
2. The purpose of this lesson is to pinpoint the true standard of authority today.

Discussion
I. **Christ Has All Authority**
   A. "And Jesus came and spoke to them, saying, 'All _____ has been given to Me in heaven and on earth'" (Matt. 28:18).
   B. God speaks to us today through Christ. "God, who at various times and in various ways spoke in time past to the fathers by the prophets, has in these last days spoken to us by His _____, whom He has appointed heir of all things, through whom also He made the worlds" (Heb. 1:1-2).
   C. Christ's authority is revealed to us in the New Testament. "If anyone thinks himself to be a prophet, or spiritual, let him acknowledge that the things which I _____ to you are the _____ of the Lord" (1 Cor. 14:37).
   D. The Bible is God's final and complete revelation to man (2 Tim. 3:16-17; Jude 3).

II. **Strictness in God's Law**
   A. God means what He says and says what He means! "You shall _____ add to the word which I command you, nor _____ it, that you may keep the commandments of the Lord your God which I command you" (Deut. 4:2).
   B. John said, "Whoever transgresses and does not _____ in the doctrine of Christ does not have God. He who abides in the doctrine of Christ has both the Father and the Son" (2 John 9).

C. Examples of God's strictness:
1. Adam and Eve ate of the fruit and were driven from the garden of Eden (Gen. 2:16-17; chapter 3).
2. Nadab and Abihu offered strange fire which they had no authority to do and were killed (Lev. 10:1-2).
3. Moses struck the rock and was not allowed to enter the promised land (Num. 20:7-12).
4. Uzzah touched the ark of the covenant, that was not to be touched, and died (2 Sam. 6:6-7).

III. God's Will Can Be Understood
A. Many think that the Bible cannot be understood. But we are commanded to understand it. "By which, when you read, you may _____ my knowledge in the mystery of Christ" (Eph. 3:4). "Therefore do not be unwise, but _____ what the will of the Lord is" (Eph. 5:17).
B. Do you think that God would give us a book to read, believe, and obey, but then make it too hard to understand?
C. This does not mean that the Bible reads as a first grade reader. It simply means that, with study, you can understand what God expects of you without some special anointing of God.

IV. False Standards of Authority
A. Let's take a look at some false standards of authority that many appeal to in religion.
1. **Conscience.**
   a. In religious matters, many people just let their conscience be their guide. Conscience is that which tells us whether we are doing right or wrong, based upon what we have been taught.
   b. Personal experiences and feelings can lead one astray, yet many are guided by them. Solomon said, "There is a _____ that _____ right to a man, But its end is the way of _____" (Prov. 14:12).
   c. The apostle Paul was guided by his conscience (Acts 23:1), but he did many things which were religiously wrong. "Indeed, I myself _____ I must do many things _____ to the name of Jesus of Nazareth" (Acts 26:9).
2. **The wisdom of men.**
   a. Men can be wrong! Our faith must not be in our own thinking, nor in the wisdom of others. "That your _____

should not be in the wisdom of _____ but in the power of God" (1 Cor. 2:5).
  b. God's ways and man's ways are different. "For since, in the wisdom of God, the world through _____ did not _____ God. . ." (1 Cor. 1:21). "O Lord, I know the way of man is not in himself; It is _____ in man who walks to _____ his own steps" (Jer. 10:23).
  c. This will eliminate all man-made creed books that almost every denomination has. God's only creed is the Bible!
3. **The majority.**
  a. The majority of people can be wrong.
  b. Just because the majority may do a thing does not make it right. There were only eight persons saved in the ark (1 Pet. 3:20).
  c. "Enter by the narrow gate; for wide is the gate and broad is the way that leads to destruction, and there are _____ who go in by it. Because narrow is the gate and difficult is the way which leads to life, and there are _____ who find it" (Matt. 7:13-14).
  d. The Lord's people have always been the few (Deut. 7:7).
4. **Parents.**
  a. Many want to follow tradition handed down by their parents. Belonging to a church simply because one's parents did is going by a false standard.
  b. "He who loves _____ or _____ more than Me is not worthy of Me. . ." (Matt. 10:37).
  c. Christianity is an individual thing. You must examine the Bible for yourself and do what it teaches.
  d. Paul was involved in religious error because he followed tradition. ". . . I persecuted the church of God beyond measure . . . being more exceedingly zealous for the _____ of my fathers" (Gal. 1:13-14).
5. **The law of Moses.**
  a. Many fail to realize that the law of Moses is not our standard of authority in religion today. It served its purpose and has been done away.
  b. The law was added because of transgressions, _____ the seed should come (Gal. 3:19). Who is identified as the seed? _____ (Gal. 3:16).

      c. "Having wiped out the handwriting of requirements that was against us, which was contrary to us. And He has _____ it _____ of the way. . ." (Col. 2:14).
      d. See also Galatians 3:23-25; Ephesians 2:15; and Hebrews 8:7-9.
      e. This is the reason we do not keep the Sabbath, burn incense, offer animal sacrifices, and do other things they did under the law of Moses.
      f. It was the death of Christ that took the law of Moses away and put into force the New Testament (Heb. 9:16-17).
      g. The Old Testament is still beneficial for us today. We learn how God deals with people and receive many moral lessons from it (Rom. 15:4; 1 Cor. 10:11). It is inspired of God and we believe what it says. We just do not live under the same specific laws they did.
  B. False standards of authority keep people from understanding the Lord's will for us today.

Conclusion

1. The standard of authority for today is Christ's will or the New Testament.
2. In the judgment to come, we will be judged by the gospel of Christ (John 12:48; Rom. 2:16).

Lesson 2

God's Plan for Saving Man

Introduction
1. Man is lost in sin and cannot save himself by himself alone (Jer. 10:23). Therefore, God has made salvation available to all men (Titus 2:11).
2. Men teach many conflicting ideas about salvation, but God's plan for saving man is simple and clearly revealed in the New Testament.

Discussion
I. Why We Need a Plan
   A. **Because man is a sinner.** "For _____ have _____ and fall short of the glory of God" (Rom. 3:23). ". . .sin is lawlessness" (1 John 3:4). Sins are not inherited, but are committed as we violate God's law.
   B. **Because sin leads to death.** "For the wages of sin is _____" (Rom. 6:23). The "death" here is spiritual, that is, eternally separated from God in hell. To avoid this death our sins must be forgiven by God.
   C. **Because goodness alone does not save.**
      1. Man has to obey the Lord to be saved. Goodness alone did not save Cornelius. From Acts 10:2, list four things which show that Cornelius was a good moral man. _____
      _____
      _____
      2. We know that Cornelius was not a saved man for he had to hear "_____ by which you and all your household will be saved" (Acts 11:14). Only Christ saves, not morality alone.
   D. **Because man must do what the Lord commands.**
      1. Jesus said, "Not everyone who says to Me, 'Lord, Lord,' shall enter the kingdom of heaven, but he who _____ the will of My Father in heaven" (Matt. 7:21).

2. Jesus is "the author of eternal salvation to all who _____ Him" (Heb. 5:9).
3. Man, being a free moral agent, has the right to choose to obey the Lord and be saved, or to reject what the Lord said and be ". . . _____ with everlasting destruction from the presence of the Lord and from the glory of His power" (2 Thess. 1:9).

II. **The Divine Side in Salvation**
   A. There are some things that God has already done for us to make salvation available.
      1. **God sent His Son.** "For God so loved the world that He _____ His only begotten Son, that whoever believes in Him should not perish but have everlasting life" (John 3:16).
      2. **God bestowed His grace.** "For by _____ you have been saved through faith, and that not of yourselves; it is the gift of God, not of works, lest anyone should boast" (Eph. 2:8-9).
      3. **Jesus shed His blood.** "In Him we have redemption through His _____, the forgiveness of sins, according to the riches of His grace" (Eph. 1:7). "For the Son of man has come to seek and to _____ that which was lost" (Luke 19:10).
      4. **The Holy Spirit revealed God's will to man.** "How that by revelation He made known to me the mystery (as I have briefly written already, by which, when you read, you may understand my knowledge in the mystery of Christ), which in other ages was not made known to the sons of men, as it has now been _____ by the Spirit to His holy apostles and prophets" (Eph. 3:3-5). This revelation is the gospel. "For I am not ashamed of the _____ of Christ: for it is the power of God unto _____ . . ." (Rom. 1:16). This is how the Spirit works today, not by miraculous intervention.
   B. God has done His part and requires that man do his part to complete the process of salvation.

III. **The Human Side in Salvation**
   A. **Hear the gospel.** ". . .This is My beloved Son, in whom I am well pleased. _____ Him!" (Matt. 17:5). Romans 10:17 teaches us that hearing the word will produce _____. Faith is not zapped into your heart mysteriously.

B. **Faith in Christ.** ". . . for if you do not _____ that I am He, you will die in your sins" (John 8:24). Some teach that man is saved by faith alone, but the New Testament does not teach that faith or anything else by itself will save us. James said, "You see then that a man is justified by works, and _____ by faith only" (James 2:24). The faith that saves is the type of faith like Noah and Abraham had—one which leads to obedience.

C. **Repentance of sins.** "Truly, these times of ignorance God overlooked, but now commands all men everywhere to _____" (Acts 17:30). An example of repentance is found in Matthew 21:28-31. What did the boy do when he repented? _____

_____
We must change from the things of the world (sin) to the things of Christ (righteousness). This is not perfection, but a sincere desire of our will to live right.

D. **The confession.** "Therefore whoever _____ _____ before men, him I will also confess before My Father who is in heaven" (Matt. 10:32). "That if you _____ with your mouth the Lord Jesus and believe in your heart that God has raised Him from the dead, you will be saved" (Rom. 10:9). There is an example of the confession being made in Acts 8:36-38. He did not confess his sins. What did he confess? _____

_____

E. **Baptism.** "He who believes and is _____ will be _____. . ." (Mark 16:16). Peter said, "There is also an antitype which now _____ _____ us. . ." (1 Pet. 3:21).
   1. The purpose of baptism is to _____ away sins (Acts 22:16); or _____ the remission of sins (Acts 2:38). This is why a person should want to be baptized.
   2. Baptism is not just "an outward sign of an inward grace," but is an act of obedience required of God in order to become a Christian.
   3. Baptism is a burial or immersion in water; not a pouring or sprinkling. The word "baptism" itself means immersion. "Or do you not know that as many of us as were _____ into Christ Jesus were baptized into His death? Therefore we were _____ with Him through baptism into death. . ." (Rom. 6:3-4). Notice, in Acts 8:36-39, that they came unto water, went down into the water, the baptism took place, and then they came up out of the water. Here is a vivid description of immersion.

Home Bible Study

4. It is at this point that the blood of Jesus washes away our sins and we get into Christ (Gal. 3:27).
5. You can clearly see that baptism is essential to salvation.

F. **Be faithful.** After one has obeyed the gospel, he then is added to the _____ (Acts 2:47). As a Christian and member of the Lord's church, one must remain faithful in worshipping God, purity of life, and working for the Lord. ". . .Be _____ until death, and I will give you the crown of life" (Rev. 2:10). One must be ". . . _____, immoveable, always abounding in the work of the Lord..." (1 Cor. 15:58).

1. Many Christians are not faithful. They sin and slip back into the world. Their condition is described in Galatians 5:4 as, "_____ from grace," for they did not continue to obey the Lord (Col. 1:23).
2. When a Christian sins (and they do), God requires him to repent, confess his sin, and pray for forgiveness (Acts 8:13-22; 1 John 1:9).
3. We all make mistakes. When we sin publicly, we need to make public confession. Private sins can be taken care of privately, between God and ourselves.
4. When a Christian becomes unfaithful and does not obey, he "walks disorderly" and the Bible says, ". . . note that person and do not keep _____ with him, that he may be ashamed" (2 Thess. 3:6-15).

Conclusion
1. This is not our plan, but rather God's plan for all mankind. Since salvation belongs to the Lord (Ps. 3:8), we have no right to change the plan He gave to save us.
2. We need to simply believe and obey it today.

Lesson 3

The Church

Introduction
1. In the midst of so many religious bodies teaching conflicting doctrines, one finds himself with the difficult task of locating the true church.
2. We can easily locate the right church by examining the distinct marks of identification of the church as revealed in the New Testament, and then finding the one today that has these same marks of identification.

Discussion
I. **Salvation and the Church**
   A. We see the importance of the church, when we realize that salvation and the church are connected. One cannot be saved outside of the church. Jesus is the ". . . _____ of the body" (Eph. 5:23). "And the Lord added to the church daily those who were being _____" (Acts 2:47).
   B. To be in the church is the same as being in Christ (Eph. 1:22-23), where salvation is (2 Tim. 2:10).

II. **Some Things the Church Is Not**
   A. Sometimes we can better understand what a thing is if we first know what it is not.
      1. **The church is not a material building.** "God, who made the world and everything in it, since He is Lord of heaven and earth, does not dwell in temples made with _____" (Acts 17:24). What was it that came upon the church in Acts 5:11? _____ The church is a group of Christians; not a physical building.
      2. **The church is not a social club.** "For the kingdom of God is not _____ and _____, but righteousness and peace and joy in the Holy Spirit" (Rom. 14:17).

Home Bible Study 15

It is not the business of the church to be involved in social affairs, such as providing entertainment and recreation.
3. **The church is not a denomination.** The church of the Lord is not a part of anything, as "denomination" implies. The church of the Bible is a non-denominational body.

B. Now that we know what the church is not, let's notice some things the Bible teaches about the church.

III. Some Things the Bible Teaches about the Church

A. **The church was planned by God.** The church was in the "_____ purpose of God" (Eph. 3:10-11). The church was not just an afterthought, but planned by God from the beginning.

B. **The church was predicted in the Old Testament.** The prophets of the Old Testament predicted that the church would be established. One outstanding prophecy is that of Isaiah 2:2-3. "Now it shall come to pass in the _____ days that the mountain of the Lord's _____ shall be established on the top of the mountains, and shall be exalted above the hills; and _____ _____ shall flow to it . . . for out of Zion shall go forth the law, and the word of the Lord from Jerusalem."

C. **The church is revealed in the New Testament.** The prophecy of Isaiah 2 is fulfilled in the establishment of the church as recorded in Acts 2. Read Acts 2 and notice the fulfillment of Isaiah's prophecy. The apostles were guided by the Holy Spirit to preach the gospel, men heard it, believed it, and obeyed it. As a result, the Lord "added to the _____ daily those who were being _____" (Acts 2:47). For the first time the church is said to be in existence. Always before this time, the church was spoken of as being in the future. This was shortly after Christ arose from the dead around AD 33.

D. **The church was built by Christ.** Jesus said, ". . . and on this rock I will _____ My church. . ." (Matt. 16:18). Christ is the foundation of the church (1 Cor. 3:11). Any church built by somebody else is not the Lord's church.

E. **The church is headed by Christ.** Paul said, "And He [Christ] is the _____ of the body, the _____ . . ." (Col. 1:18). Christ is the Head and the church is His body. Since this is true, the church must be in subjection to its Head, Christ. "Therefore, just as the church is _____ to Christ, so let the wives be to their own husbands in everything" (Eph. 5:24).

The church has no man for its head here on the earth. Christ has all authority (Matt. 28:18), which leaves none for anyone else to make religious laws.

F. **The church was purchased by the blood of Christ.** The great value of the church can be seen when we realize that it took the blood of Christ to purchase it. Paul told the Ephesian elders, "Therefore take heed to yourselves and to all the flock . . . to shepherd the church of God which He _____ with His own _____" (Acts 20:28). Peter said that we were purchased "with the precious _____ of Christ" (1 Pet. 1:18-19).

G. **The church is Christ possessed.** The church belongs to Christ. There is no exclusive name given to the Lord's church. It is certainly proper to refer to the Lord's church by the names given in the Scriptures. Paul said, "The churches of Christ greet you" (Rom. 16:16). A church that does not wear the name of Christ must not belong to Him. The members of the church belong to Christ and thus wear the name God gave His people to wear, that is, Christian (Acts 11:26; Isa. 62:2; 1 Pet. 4:16). The Bible will make you only a Christian; nothing else. Let us respect Christ by wearing only His name for the church.

H. **The church is independently organized.** Every church in New Testament times was independent of every other church. Elders were ordained in "every church" (Acts 14:23). Each church had its own elders, deacons, and members. Paul's letter to the Philippians was addressed to "all the _____ in Christ Jesus who are in Philippi, with the _____ and _____" (Phil. 1:1). Elders and deacons are men who meet qualifications laid down in 1 Timothy 3. The elders oversee the flock; only their own (1 Pet. 5:1-3), while the deacons serve the local church. Elders are also called bishops or pastors (not the preachers). There is no organization larger or smaller than the local church through which the church is to function. State and nationwide church groups are foreign to the Bible.

I. **The church is guided by the Bible.** The Bible completely furnishes us with all that we need religiously (2 Tim. 3:16-17). The church has no other creed.

J. **The church worships in truth.** Worship must be as God has directed or it is vain (Matt. 15:9; John 4:24). More about worship in our next lesson.

K. **The church teaches the Lord's plan of salvation.** In our last lesson, we learned that God's plan for saving us involves hearing, faith, repentance, confession, baptism, and being faithful. A church that teaches anything other than this is not the Lord's church.

IV. The Work of the Church
A. The work of the church is given to us by Christ and is of a spiritual nature. It involves basically three things:
   1. Preaching the gospel (1 Thess. 1:8; Matt. 28:19-20).
   2. Helping needy saints (Rom. 15:25-26; 1 Tim. 5:16,).
   3. Teaching Christians (Acts 20:32; Eph. 4:11-16).
B. The church can use its money to provide for these things. The church has no business being involved in social affairs, social reforms, political affairs, or providing entertainment and recreation. These are things which belong in the home or to the individual (1 Cor. 11:22-34).

V. The Lord Established One Church
A. The New Testament teaches that there is only one body. "But now indeed there are many members, yet _____ body" (1 Cor. 12:20). "There is _____ body and one Spirit, just as you were called in one hope of your calling" (Eph. 4:4).
B. There is one body and the body is the church (Col. 1:18). If there is only one body and the body is the church, how many churches are there? _____

Conclusion
1. We have learned about the church of the Bible, the Lord's church. Jesus established His church to provide salvation. It is vital then that we be a part of the Lord's church.
2. We encourage you to search for a church that has these marks of identification. Investigate the local church of Christ. Many churches claim to be true, but simply do not follow the Bible in these matters.

Lesson 4

The Worship of the Church

Introduction
1. The modern philosophy in worship is that a person can worship God any way that he wants to. Legally one can, but to please God and be acceptable unto Him, our worship must be on God's terms, as Christ has directed.
2. Our worship must be unto God only (Matt. 4:10). The Old Testament is full of examples where worship was misdirected or wrongly offered. In Exodus 20:3, God said, "You shall have no other gods before Me." This lesson is designed to teach us how to properly worship God today.

Discussion
I. **Worship: True or Vain?**
   A. **Worship can be in vain.** "And in _____ they _____ Me, teaching as doctrines the commandments of men" (Matt. 15:9). These people were worshipping God, but it was vain or to no avail, because it was not as God directed.
      1. Read the story of Nadab and Abihu from Leviticus 10:1-2. They died because they offered strange fire in their sacrifice (worship) which God had commanded them _____. They may have thought they could worship God with any fire, or maybe the strange fire was better, after all God had not said they could not use it. But God would not accept it, for He had not authorized it.
      2. This same principle is taught in 2 John 9-11 and Colossians 3:17. Our worship must be by Jesus' authority. To go beyond is to not have God.
   B. **True worship.** "God is Spirit, and those who worship Him must worship in _____ and _____" (John 4:24).

1. To worship in spirit is to worship from the heart. It involves understanding, meaning, and feeling. This is the attitude of acceptable worship (Matt. 15:8).
2. To worship in truth is to worship by the teachings of the truth, the Word of God (John 17:17). This is the standard for acceptable worship.

II. **Items of New Testament Worship**
   A. To fully worship God, we must assemble with the church. "Not forsaking the _____ of ourselves together . . ." (Heb. 10:25).
   B. Here are the methods of worship we are to use:
      1. **Teaching**
         a. "_____ them to observe all things that I have commanded you . . ." (Matt. 28:20). Who are the ones to be taught in this verse? _____ _____
         b. "It is written in the prophets, 'And they shall all be _____ _____ by God. . .'" (John 6:45).
         c. The early Christians "continued steadfastly in the apostles' _____." (Acts 2:42). Doctrine is teaching.
         d. This is why Bible classes are offered and sermons are preached.
         e. We see a good example of the church meeting for worship and Paul preaching to them in Acts 20:7.
      2. **Prayer**
         a. "_____ always with all prayer and supplication in the Spirit. . ." (Eph. 6:18).
         b. "And they continued steadfastly in the apostles' doctrine and fellowship, in the breaking of bread, and in _____" (Acts 2:42).
         c. "Peter was therefore kept in prison, but constant _____ was offered to God for him by the _____" (Acts 12:5).
      3. **Singing**
         a. There are two kinds of music: vocal and mechanical. Read these passages to see which one is authorized by Christ.
         b. "Speaking to one another in psalms and _____ and spiritual songs, _____ and making _____ in your _____ to the Lord" (Eph. 5:19).
         c. "Let the word of Christ dwell in you richly in all wisdom, teaching and admonishing one another in psalms and

_____ and spiritual songs, _____ with grace in your _____ to the Lord" (Col. 3:16).
   d. Other Scriptures: Matthew 26:30; Mark 14:26; Acts 16:25; Romans 15:9; 1 Corinthians 14:15; Hebrews 2:12; 13:15; James 5:13.
   e. From these Scriptures it is easy to see that the only kind of music Christ has directed us to use is vocal. That's the only kind the New Testament churches used and it is the only kind that we should use today. Notice also that we are to all sing to each other, and not have a choir to sing to or for us.
4. **The Lord's supper**
   a. "And they continued steadfastly in the apostles' doctrine and fellowship, in the _____ of _____, and in prayers" (Acts 2:42).
   b. Please read Acts 20:7 and then fill in the following:
      (1) What did the Christians assemble for at Troas? _____
      (2) When God told Israel to remember the Sabbath day to keep it holy (Exod. 20:8), how often did He expect them to keep the Sabbath day holy? Every Sabbath day, or any Sabbath day they chose? _____ _____
      (3) In the same connection, when the disciples at Troas came together on the first day of the week to break bread, how often did they take the Lord's supper? _____
      (4) Can you imagine a church meeting on the first day of the week and then leaving out the memorial of Christ? The communion is to be taken every week.
   c. Read 1 Corinthians 11:23-30 and fill in the following:
      (1) List the two elements of the Lord's supper. _____ _____ and _____ _____ _____.
      (2) What is the purpose of the Lord's supper? _____ _____
5. **Giving**
   a. "On the first day of the week let each one of you _____ _____ _____ , storing up as he may _____, that there be no collections when I come" (1 Cor. 16:2).

b. ". . .He who sows sparingly will also reap sparingly, and he who sows _____ will also reap bountifully. So let each one give as he _____ in his heart, not grudgingly or of necessity; for God loves a _____ giver" (2 Cor. 9:6-7).
c. In the Old Testament, the Jews were required to tithe or give a tenth to the Lord. But from these passages, has God bound any certain amount on us today? _____
d. This is the only way that a church can raise money. There is no authorization for pie suppers, door-to-door soliciting, bingo parties, dinners, or going into business to raise money. Notice also that the day for the contribution is the _____ day of week (1 Cor. 16:2).

Conclusion
1. We have learned that worship must be on God's terms to be acceptable. Also, we have learned what those terms are, as revealed in the New Testament. Just because something pleases us, and we want to worship God that way, is no sign that it is pleasing to God. Let us be content to worship only in these ways and leave out everything else.
2. Worship is not entertainment. There are no special holy days mentioned in the Bible for special worship services for us today (like Christmas and Easter). Every Sunday is alike in our worship unto God.

www.ingramcontent.com/pod-product-compliance
Lightning Source LLC
Chambersburg PA
CBHW071958060426
42444CB00044B/3165